BLOOM'S BOUQUET OF
IMAGINARY WORDS

BLOOM'S BOUQUET OF
IMAGINARY WORDS

Jeffrey and Carole Bloom

Illustrations by Steven Noble

BLACK DOG
& LEVENTHAL
PUBLISHERS
NEW YORK

ISBN 1-57912-451-8
Library of Congress Cataloging-in-Publication Data
Bloom, Jeffrey.
Bloom's bouquet of imaginary words / Jeffrey Bloom & Carole Bloom.
p. cm.
Includes bibliographical references and index.
ISBN 1-57912-451-8 (alk. paper)
1. English language—Terms and phrases—Humor. 2. English language—Humor. 3.
Vocabulary—Humor. I. Title: Bouquet of imaginary words. II. Bloom, Carole (Carole Wilson)
III. Title.
PN6231.W64B46 2004
818'.602—dc22
2004022393

Book design: Scott Citron
Manufactured in the United States of America

Published by
Black Dog & Leventhal Publishers, Inc.
151 West 19th Street
New York, New York 10011

Distributed by
Workman Publishing Company
708 Broadway
New York, New York 10003

b d f g e c a

To our wonderful friend Shane Briant—
international film star, novelist, screenwriter,
raconteur, bon vivant—who gave credence to this
project with his *credit curd*. And to Carole's father Al,
who taught her that the most important word in the
English language is *now*.

CONTENTS

Shelfish
A self-involved crustacean

INTRODUCTION

EVELYN WAUGH SAID, AMONG OTHER THINGS, "One's vocabulary needs constant fertilizing or it will die." He may have been right about that. But it's possible that it never occurred to Mr. Waugh that by merely adding, deleting, or changing a single letter, we can significantly expand the *meaning* of words.

For example, if we start with the word *destination* and substitute the letter *u* for the letter *e*, we can create a new word—*dustination*—and a valuable new definition: Where dirt ends up.

Simply by substituting the letter *w* for the letter *r*, a large, thick-skinned, bitchy mammal becomes a *whinoceros*.

As you can see, in the creation of the new word, the original word hasn't been lost, but in a way made to blossom.

The addition of a modest *r* makes a small bit of joy received from doing something well a *satisfraction*.

The words bloom, we realized. Like our family name. Like flowers in a garden. And our accommodating language is enhanced by this new specificity.

For every new word we've created there are surely a hundred more waiting to be born (*Question: What do you call a chubby bird? Answer: A pugeon*), and we encourage our readers to stimulate their minds by inventing their own.

Remember to stick to the simple rules:

1. Be creative.

2. Don't be afraid to be silly.

3. Know that it's both a challenge and a reward.

—Jeffrey and Carole Bloom

"It's a weak mind that can think of only one way to spell a word."

—Mark Twain

PUGEONS & PIGAMISTS
(ANIMALS, PETS, & PESTS)

Whinoceros
A large, thick-skinned, bitchy mammal

Compromice
Rats that settle for less

Alphapet
Top Dog

Anonymouse
Rodent with no name

Animall
Zoo

Catthroat
A ruthless kitty

Cabinewt
A salamander's vacation home

Kangaroom
Where baby marsupials sleep

Curtoon
An animated short film featuring a mongrel dog

Shlepherd
Ewe hauler

Elephonts
Large print styles

Petreleum
A sea bird victimized by an oil spill

Tacitern
A quiet gull

Seaquins
Ornamental fish scales

Beaverage
A drink shared by semiaquatic, web-footed mammals

Preveal
First indication of a pregnant cow

Cawtious
Careful of wild crows

Fidocaine
Anesthetic for dogs

Neurosturgeon
Marine biologist

Pairadox
Twin dachshunds

Moovement
A cow pie

Limoswine
A vehicle for transporting rich pigs

Flamingoy
A gentile bird

Plachyderm
Tartar scraped from elephant tusks

Chipmonk
A small, deeply religious squirrel

Roverture
Classical barking

Roteation
Moving a nursing calf from udder to udder

Perchment
Paper in the bottom of a birdcage

Craneum
A bird brain

Meenk
A docile animal raised for its fur

Mouseum
A place where Mickey and Minnie memorabilia is displayed

Shyena
Bashful scavenger

Steerilize
To neuter a bull

Pigamist
A swine of a swine

Paultry
Inferior chickens

Polligraph
Device used to detect a lying parrot

Fortuitousk
The chance discovery of a long, protruding tooth

Talismane
Good luck charm made of horsehair

Lachrymoose
Bullwinkle after the television series was cancelled

Shamster
A fake gerbil

Pandamonium
Excitement over a new arrival at the zoo

Cheatah
A deceitful cat

Racoonteur
A small, bushy-tailed, anecdotal mammal

Clamity
*A mollusk's profound sense of impending
doom as the water is boiled*

Gangsteer
A member of a herd of violent, castrated bovines

Shysteer
An unscrupulous gangsteer with a law degree

Catterpillar
A tall scratching post for felines

Epooch
A day in a dog's life

Glibbon
A smart-aleck monkey

Bleatant
In ewe face

Eskimoo
A cow indigenous to Canada or Alaska

Burkat
Loose garment used to cover female Muslim kittens

Beastitudes
Blessings for animals

Deerriere
A buck's butt

Moraytorium
An authorized waiting period for the capture of eels

Goombaa
Italian sheep

Damphibian
Perpetually moist frog

Marsoupial
Australian pet food broth sold in pouch form

Pugeon
Chubby bird

Magnanimouse
A noble rodent

Squarrel
A dispute between arboreal rodents

Pignoble
A stoat with a poor pedigree

Domasticated
A wild animal trained to chew politely

Sarcoophagus
An empty eggshell discovered in a hatchery

Amplifly
A winged insect that buzzes loudly

Identifly
A winged insect recognized on sight

Pacifly
A winged insect that keeps peace among its kind

Testifly
A winged insect called as a witness

Comediant
A funny insect

Whornet
A large, promiscuous female wasp

Verman
A whornet's pimp

Flamboyants
Big, flashy insects

Paraspite
*An organism that thrives off a host even
though it would rather not*

Pestimistic
*Believing that insects and rodents
will inherit the earth*

"*We should have a great fewer disputes in the world if words were taken for what they are: the signs of our ideas only, and not for things themselves.*"

—John Locke

PLUMPKINS AND GRIMLETS
(FOOD & DRINK)

Mayonnaisle
At a salad bar, a passage between dressings

Sorcercress
Greens for a female wizard

Credit curd
A way to charge cheese

Breakfist
Morning karate injury

Kiltchen
Where Scotsmen prepare meals

Containters
Packages for spoiled food

Rapberry juice
Hip hop drink

Suppervisor
Head waiter

Fonduel
Food fight

Crestaurant
Place to eat at the top of a hill

Jurkey
Dehydrated Thanksgiving leftovers

Pinthouse
Top floor of an English pub

Coiffee
Refreshment served at a beauty salon

Punishmeat
*Being made to sit at the table until
you've finished your pot roast*

Balonely
Sandwich meat for singles

Pearvert
A kinky fruit

Calfeteria
A self-serve restaurant specializing in veal dishes

Psychedeli
Restaurant where Timothy Leary ate pastrami sandwiches

Paeola
*Bribe paid to a Spanish chef for preparing
a special rice and seafood dish*

Cloysters
Shellfish enjoyed by nuns

Kohlrabbi
A kind of cabbage served at some synagogues

Meatropolis
Kansas City or Chicago

Barebecue
Nudist colony picnic

Bardbecue
Elizabethan playreading and alfresco supper

Brrbecue
Outdoor grilling on a sub-zero day

Ghoulash
Beef stew favored by Hungarian grave-robbers

Poortion
A dinner serving at a homeless shelter

Imbible
To sip sherry while reading the scripture

Tequilag
The moment before inebriation

Grimlet
A vodka drink served with fierce determination

Creoleo
Louisiana margarine

Psalami
A sausage referenced in sacred songs

Stubmarine
Small hoagie

Sommeliar
An equivocating wine steward

Parslimonious
Trying to save money on garnish

Pieneer
Originator of encrusted baked fruit

Compotition
A dessert-making contest

Supperb
A fantastic dinner

Plumpkin
Rotund squash

Gasparagus
Flatulence-inducing vegetable

Expresto
Instant Italian coffee

Osteopotrosis
*A method of braising beef for many hours
so that the bones become brittle*

Liverated
Free from having to eat pâté

Escargo
A shipment of small snails

Luftwaffle
German air force traditional breakfast

Hempanada
Latin American pastry high in fiber

Dromedairy
An Arabian factory for processing milk products from camels

Dime Sum
Dumplings, ten for a dollar

Repoachful
Expressing consternation with Eggs Benedict

Raſtaurateur
Owner-operator of a Jamaican restaurant

Gumboa
Louisiana snake stew

Raisin d'être
The justification for the existence of dried fruit

Lowcality
The area of a supermarket set aside for diet foods

Persnickerty
Fussy about a candy bar

Samebuca
Brands of flavored liqueurs whose tastes are indistinguishable

Consederable
The amount of food served on Passover

Flaboratory
Research center for diet products

Minustrone
A thick vegetable soup lacking beans or pasta

Martiny
Small cocktail

Ex-Lox
Née salmon

Cashrew
An evil nut

Adiptation
Becoming accustomed to chips and guacamole

Stuffocate
To die from overeating

Prigatoni
Obnoxiously over-elegant pasta

Coppellini
Pasta served at a police station

Brigatoni
Pasta served to sailors who go AWOL

Lunguini
Pasta preferred by non-smokers

Fussilli
Prissy pasta

Frettuccine
Pasta for worriers

Pappaldelle
The Pope's pasta

Spurghetti
Cowboy pasta

"*The difference between the right word and the almost right word is the difference between lightning and a lightning bug.*"

—Mark Twain

FROSHBITE & FROLLICLES
(MEDICINE)

Lidocanine
Anesthetic for dogs

eMoil
Someone who performs circumcisions on the Internet

Bracist
*Having an irrational hostility toward
orthodontic appliances*

Immuknology
The study of teenage resistance to formal education

Handiclap
Anatomical abnormality resulting in an inability to applaud

Osteoplath
Skeleton of a dead poet

Prophylaptic
*A device used to prevent disease while
sitting on someone's lap*

Nazit
Hitler youth blemish

Lamputate
Cut the lights

Practologist
Doctor who takes a nuts-and-bolts approach to the rectum

Suturated
Having many stitches

Discomboobulation
A plastic surgeon's error

Frollicle
Small, mischievous lymph node

Malecule
The absolute smallest part of a man's body

Pilliterate
A pharmacist unable to read doctors' prescriptions

Genietalia
Parts of the human body stimulated by polishing a lamp

Cockooned
Not circumcised

Scannery
An MRI lab

Plumpectomy
Liposuction

Coronairy
An in-flight heart attack

Faulter
To incorrectly predict an earthquake

Porcuspine
A protruding vertebrae

Overtebra
*An orthopedic undergarment providing
support for a porcuspine*

Dissadvantage
To humiliate someone with a handicap

Well-endowned
Man with excessive pubic hair

Sircumcision
Cutting the foreskin of a knight

Mountainear
Echoing malady that afflicts climbers

Deviaunt
The behaviorally challenged sister of one's father or mother

Sherpes
A skin disease common to Tibetan mountain-climbers

Internnational
A young, traveling doctor

Pumpernuckle
Repetitive injury from drawing water from a well

Froshbite
Freezing college newbie's condition

Clausetrophobia
Fear of making changes in a formal document

Cellebration
Moment of conception

Palamine
Poison ivy lotion shared with a friend

Nocturinal
A glow-in-the-dark vessel for nighttime use

Contracaption
A written accompaniment to an illustration of a diaphragm

Palanoia
Irrational suspicion of a friend

Keeptomania
A relentless neurotic impulse to save everything

Anusthetic
Preparation H

Manorectic
A guy with no appetite

Meloncholy
Fruit of the Gloom

Doledrums
A feeling of despondency after eating canned pineapple

Intrinsick
Fundamentally ill

Streptomychin
An antibiotic used in the treatment of
bacterial infections of the lower jaw

Minuscale
An extremely small flake of dead skin, such as dandruff

Mariache
Pain afflicting strolling Mexican folk musicians

Lobstetrics
A branch of veterinary medicine concerned
with marine crustaceans

Exfooliate
A procedure in which the brain is cleansed of dead cells

Athletick
Stress-induced facial twitch caused by Olympic competition

Fastigue
The rapid onset of extreme tiredness

Laxactive
*The productive effect of a medicine
designed to relieve constipation*

Mallnutrition
*A severe dietary imbalance resulting from
overeating at shopping center fast-food stalls*

Hybride
A hermaphrodite on his/her wedding day

Whiskhers
Female chin hairs

Waftermath
A lingering odor after a passage of gas

Frostrate
The position of a body in a morgue freezer

Procrustinator
A baker who habitually puts off making pie shells

Loxative
Smoked Ex-Lax

Parchmint
Lozenge for dry throat

Lunartic
A twitch when the moon is full

Harbinge
The announcement of an intention to indulge excessively

Banalgesic
A drug acting to relieve boredom

Briskit
Instruments used by a moil to make a prime cut

Hangovert
*A public display of the disagreeable physical
effects of heavy consumption of alcohol*

Manxiety
Fear of short-tailed cats

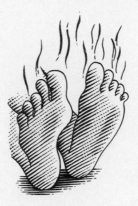

Halitoesis
Smelly feet

Stunburn
A reddish-brown mark left on the skin as a result of an electric shock administered by a police officer's weapon

Pieriodontics
*A branch of medical engineering that deals with
the supporting structures of dental bridges*

Pediatricks
Child doctor's technique to distract fearful patients

Blotulism
Breaking out with a spotty rash after eating tainted food

"The two most engaging powers of an author are to make new things familiar and familiar things new."

—Samuel Johnson

SEXCUSES & EJOCULATION
(SEX)

Ejoculation
Telling jokes during a sexual climax

Whoresale
A way for prostitutes to purchase affordable condoms

Testickle
Making one's partner laugh during foreplay

Sucktion
Fellatio

Prostitote
Hooker's handbag

Maturbation
Growing old enough to please oneself

Scathouse
A home for jazz-singing prostitutes

Celebath
Avoiding private parts while washing

Princest
Sexual relations with a royal-blood relative

Sexclamation
Shouting out during lovemaking

Sexaggeration
Saying "Oooh, it's so big!" during lovemaking

Sexcuse
Saying "Not tonight, I have a headache."

Strumpeter
A horn-playing street walker

Promisacuity
The ability to remember every detail of an illicit affair

Armadildo
A plated vibrator

Voyear
One who gets sexual gratification from eavesdropping

Sexpectant
Anticipating the first night of a honeymoon

Testoysterone
A hormone that stimulates the development
of sexual characteristics in mollusks

Aphrodisiact
Pretending to be aroused after eating oysters

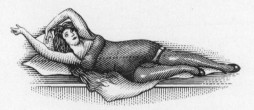

Whorizontal
A prostitute's favorite posture

Boyeur
Peeping tomgirl

Galery
A place to pick up women

Sharem
A sultan's invitation to his friends

Pornamentation
Sexually explicit decoration

Coinsummate
Pay for sex

Corresporndence
Mash notes

FIBERALS & REAPUBLICANS
(POLITICS & MILITARY)

Dicktator
Unpopular national leader

Primarry
A presidential hopeful's wedding engagement

Exxonerate
To relieve an oil company of responsibility for a spill

Preparicate
Get ready to tell a lie

Predisprosed
Prior commitment to speak

Fiberal
A left-wing liar

Pretaliation
Official justification for U.S. invasion of Iraq

Presponse
A reply to a pretaliation

Precrimination
The consequence of pretaliation and presponse

Discovert
Finding something the government has been hiding

Capitalust
D.C. free-market sex

Campain
A headache caused by stumping for office

Legitslation
Honest law-making

Reapublican
One who profits from less governmental control

Reeferendum
A popular initiative to legalize marijuana

Democarat
One who assigns weight to the concept of social equality

Cornstituency
Voters in Iowa

Anarchlist
A roster of citizens who rebel against governmental authority

Lambassador
A verbally assaultive diplomat

Presidental
A candidate's artificially enhanced smile

Senatoro
A bullish member of Congress

Lobbyfist
One who influences public officials the old-fashioned way

Referendumb
A vote on a stupid law

Failibuster
An unsuccessful attempt to delay passage of a referendumb

Elocaution
Careful speech by politically correct candidates

Tactivist
Someone who handles people with great care

Scandinaviman
A member of the Danish armed forces

Troopics
Where soldiers often go for R and R

Spentagon
A major source of U.S. military budget overruns

Polstergeist
Gallup's ghost

Tornpedo
A ruptured missile

"One must be drenched in words, literally soaked in them, to have the right ones form themselves into the proper pattern at the right moment."

—Hart Crane

PAINTALOONS & FRAGRINCE
(FASHION & GROOMING)

Spanties
Underwear size 7 or larger

Marxiskirt
A garment worn by women during the Russian revolution

Paintaloons
Baggy overalls worn by artists

Skimono
Outdoor sportswear on Mt. Fuji

Pantomine
One's own custom-tailored slacks

Flashion
A passing trend

Fragrince
A smell that brings a smile

Scentiment
Aroma that evokes heartfelt memories

Fedorca
A whale watcher's hat

Calftan
A loose-fitting robe made of young cowhide

Blandana
A boring kerchief

Misanthrobe
One who hates dressing gowns

Marathong
Undergarment worn by female long-distance runners

Leotardy
Arriving late to ballet class

Sombretro
A classic Mexican hat, back in fashion

Persuede
To coax someone to buy an expensive leather garment

Tuturial
Instructions on making a ballerina's costume

Mensweary
Tired clothing

Bathrube
A country bumpkin coverup

Ecclesilastic
Expandable waistbands for clergymen

Tryonics
Cold-storing an out-of-fashion fur in the hope
that it will one day be back in style

Aclademy
School for fashion designers

Destitote
An empty purse

Sawrong
A loose Malaysian skirt wrapped around the body incorrectly

Rigamarolex
A watch with unnecessarily complicated works

Minuskirt
A woman's skirt that's even shorter than a mini

Pauncho
*An outerwear garment generously
tailored for the overweight*

Coatillion
Wrap party

Turdban
A Mediterranean headdress made of Camel dung

Retailiation
Wholesale

Portrend
Predicting a new style

Reposetory
A place where models rest

Yarmulkey
Used to gain entrance to an orthodox Jewish haberdashery

Pradagal
A woman who spends lavishly on Italian designer purses

Holipstic
An organic cosmetic

Imprimptu
Spontaneously excessive grooming

Isotoupe
A radioactive hairpiece

Multidude
A large number of stylish men

Cleavague
Showing very little bosom

Toenality
The color scheme used by a pedicurist

Breadlocks
A hairstyle in which wet, uncombed hair is braided in the form of a traditional Jewish Sabbath challah

Booffant
A scary hairdo

"If a word in the dictionary were misspelled, how would we know?"

—Steven Wright

PROTESTUNTS & PRIMCIPALS
(RELIGION & EDUCATION)

Sermoan
A dull Sunday speech

Seremon
A burning oration from the pulpit

Prepentant
Anticipating contrition

Librerian
Someone who catalogues Uncle Remus books

Sandwitch
A desert sorceress

Cherube
A naïve angel

Massistant
Altar boy

Thormented
Annoyed by a Greek god

Sacrivice
Giving up a bad habit

Repentent
Where revival meetings are held

Gospiel
Televangelist's pitch for money

Lauditorium
Where graduation is held

Skosher
Just a bit more orthodox

Therapewtic
Sitting on a cushion during Sunday services

Sinvestigator
Church detective

Afirmament
Proof that there is a heaven

Jesuite
A fancy hotel room for a priest

Cultlery
Knives used at satanic rituals

Protestunt
A Christian trick on April Fool's Day

Primcipal
Stodgy headmistress

Soulitude
Heaven

Neaptune
Mythical god of low tides

Pulpith
The bitter heart of a sermon

Theresy
A profound commitment to what is generally accepted

Sinonym
A transgression by any name

Snacrilegious
Stealing wafers to eat after mass

Neverend
One who adamantly refuses to join the clergy

Faithfuel
Daily devotional

Hamily
A rabbi's Saturday sermon about keeping kosher

Thindu
A slender inhabitant of India

"Language ought to be the joint creation of poets and manual workers."

—George Orwell

BLANDSCAPES & VIOLINCE
(ARTS & LITERATURE)

Basshole
The tiresome string player in a jazz combo

Diseasel
To put away one's art supplies

Blandscape
A boring picture of a desert

Laborastory
A place for testing works of fiction

Confidance
What Fred and Ginger had

Tromp'bone
A musical instrument that's not really there

Voliptuous
Scarlett Johansson

Countroversy
Argument over Dracula

Megazine
A large periodical

Documeantary
A nasty, nonfiction film

Violince
A stringed instrument played with great passion

Distrauction
Raising one's paddle before it's time to bid

Vampaire
Melody familiar to blood-sucking demons

Intermazzo
Short musical composition played during Passover

Amaizon.com
A place to buy corny books

Slimbo
An acrobatic dance best performed by thin people

Scandalouse
A reporter for The Enquirer

Jestation
Period of time during which a comedian develops an act

Actcelerate
Deliver one's lines quickly

Playgiarize
Steal scenes from one production for use in another

Karaokie
A lip-synching hillbilly

Mocrame
A faux weaving

Arabasque
A Spanish-Arabian ballet move

Phantome
A book by a ghost writer

Inkspiration
A writer's need

Shakerspeare
Playwright and cabinetmaker

Fundametal
Basic enjoyment of a hard rock concert

Agentile
A Christian actor's representative

Petrifiction
A lifeless novel

Scareenwriter
An author of horror films

Proofessional
Book editor

Dialoge
A conversation in the reserved-seat section of a theatre

Solvereign
Undisputed New York Times crossword puzzle champion

Platitune
An insipid pop song

Vibralto
A countertenor tremolo

Castroto
A Cuban male singer with a very high voice

Penvious
Jealous of another writer's work

Purgastory
Dante's Inferno

Grandinose
Cyrano de Bergerac

Squintet
Five farsighted singers

Stagnote
In music, a single tone extended for a very long time

Ravelation
The surprising disclosure of an early recording of "Bolero"

Dalimation
Modern arftist

Poempous
A snobbish disdain of rhyming verse

Inkubation
*The period of time between a literary
notion and a finished work*

Satyirist
A lecherous comedian

Errasta
A list of corrected historical errors about Bob Marley

Fontierman
A pioneering graphic designer

Legerdeman
Magician David Blaine, to his fans

Apropose
An artist's model with clothes on

Correspondance
Letters from Nijinsky to Pavlova

Vagaband
Wandering minstrels

Altokocker
An elderly Jewish singer with a mid-range voice

Apropoe
Reading "The Raven" at the right time

Nanachronism
Granny attends a rave

Poortrait
A really bad painting

"Language is a process of free creation; its laws and principles are fixed, but the manner in which the principles of generation are used is free and infinitely varied."

—Noam Chomsky

COMPUTITORS & MICROCHAPS
(BUSINESS)

Entreepreneur
A chef/restaurant owner

Teenwage
Minimum salary paid to kids

Computitors
Macintosh and Dell

Harmoney
A pleasing arrangement of cash

Microchap
A very short e-fellow

Noneprofit
A very poorly run business

Verizen
Buddhist-owned communications company

Coinservationist
Someone who saves loose change in a jar

Congloomerate
Enron

Infiltrade
Penny stocks

Extravagent
A big spender

Stupoor
A state of apathy resulting from filing for bankruptcy

Cashual
Spending nonchalantly

eMolish
To destroy or tear down a website

Lincoin
A penny

Coinvert
Change dollars into cents

Prontotype
A model from which something is fashioned very quickly

Debtonation
Paid in full

Internut
Someone who's online all the time

Cadillag
A measure of sales in relation to Mercedes Benz

Curtoil
Shorten the standard work week

Fidociary
An investment broker who works like a dog

Scabriolet
A Porsche convertible driven across a picket line

Econoclast
One who attacks long-established Keynesian theories

BACHELORES & SATISFRACTION
(HUMAN NATURE)

Simptoms
Signs of weak character

Satisfraction
A small bit of joy that comes from doing well

Concentrite
To pay attention to corny things

Volunteared
Cried freely

Necesscary
Need to frighten someone

Chairity
Giving up your seat to someone who needs it more than you

Bachelore
Men's tales of the single life

Cavaleer
Disdainful look

Vehemant
Intensely emotional fellow with big muscles

Philantrophy
Award for giving to others

Freudulant
Deceitfully analytic

Benefraction
A small good deed

Forelorn
*The condition of knowing that something
depressing is about to occur*

Multimate
Wilt Chamberlain

Incandecent
Glowingly conforming to good taste and morality

Relentlass
An extremely persistent young girl

Letterbug
One who strews discarded junk mail in a public place

Ignoramuse
The guiding genius of dunces

Commiseration
Manly compassion

Hipso facto
Inherently cool

Chunky-dory
Fine, but a little overweight

Laudicrous
Laughably praiseworthy

Talcoholic
Someone who uses too much bath powder

Tacitorn
Unconvinced that silence is golden

Deafinite
Stubborn refusal to listen to any expressions of uncertainty

Improvice
Extemporaneous moral depravity

Ignorminious
Disregarding someone deserving public disgrace

Canscious
Keenly aware of recycling

Sheory
A system of ideas intended to explain womankind

Perkpetual
Forever cheerful

Whistrionics
A theatrical fit of pique during a card game

Sugjestion
Advice given as a joke

Bobstinate
Stubborn refusal to answer to the name Robert

Boysterous
*Common temperament of adolescent males when
in the company of girrulous counterparts*

Diaryhea
*An uncontrollable need to write in
one's personal journal*

Nillicit
Anything goes

"Words are not as satisfactory as we should like them to be, but, like our neighbors, we have to live with them and must make the best and not the worst of them."

—Samuel Butler

MEGAPHORS & MODIFICTION
(LANGUAGE)

Penetrite
To cut through a cliché

Prosethetics
The art of improving a bad sentence

Slanguish
*Depression induced by an inability
to use contemporary jargon*

Manswer
A gentleman's response to a question

Tradiction
Oral history

Flagrunt
Vocal disregard

Punktuation
Grammatical marks used in transcribing rock lyrics

Knewledge
Something previously learned

Scarcasm
Words that cause a deep rift

Disavowel
Refusing to acknowledge a letter of the alphabet

Puncturation
*Devaluing a literary composition by the insertion
of superfluous grammatical marks*

Heroglyphic
*Ancient picture script showing a man rescuing
a child from a burning building*

Megaphor
A figure of speech as big as all outdoors

Precurser
A harbinger of profane language

Morsaic
Small bit of code pieced together to form a message

Aficionado
A devotee of novels

Awkword
An ungainly element of speech

Repundiate
Refuse to be associated with a bad joke

Banalogy
A witless comparison between two things

Modifiction
Rewriting

Himonym
*One of two or more men having the same
name but different personalities*

Mostensible
More likely than not to be true

Deftinition
The skillful articulation of a word's exact meaning

Coynage
*Invention of a new word which is meant
to be cute but is often irritating*

Puntificate
To tell jokes in a pompous manner

Predialection
A preference for speaking with an accent

Correspondense
A ten-page letter

"*A word is dead when it is said. Some say.*
I say it just begins to live that day."

—Emily Dickinson

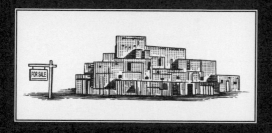

NEIGHBORES & BUNGALOOS
(HOME & GARDEN)

Shampoop
Carpet cleaning product for pet accidents

Dustination
Where dirt ends up

Bungaloo
Small, cozy bathroom

Prosperties
Very expensive homes

Schemattic
Diagram of an upstairs room

Dimestic
A not-so-bright housekeeper

Toylet
A dollhouse bathroom

Sodbluster
An arrogant farmer

Hervester
A farmer's wife

Sagriculture
Withered crops

Nomaid
A wandering housekeeper

Neighbores
Dull family next door

Presstigious
Well-ironed

Ferniture
What Tarzan sat on at home

Eterknity
Taking forever to finish making a shawl

Immanse
Larger than a house, smaller than a castle

Cornycopia
A silly Thanksgiving table decoration

Steamina
Having the energy to keep ironing

Laundromate
Clothes-washing friend

Condominimum
The smallest unit in an apartment building

Scenterpiece
Fragrant table decoration

Lederhousen
Leather-clad German homes

Pueblot
A building site in an American Indian settlement

Guardener
*Someone whose services are engaged when
a "Keep off the grass" sign fails*

Inconsoilable
Endless grieving over a stain

PARANTING & WEDUCATION
(MARRIAGE & PARENTING)

Storkage
A baby repository

Paranting
Yelling at the kids

Altarcation
Argument over wedding vows

Creemate
Plains Indian bride

Cashtrated
Having one's allowance cut off

Prymate
Nosy spouse

Succomb
Teenage boy gives in to pressure to groom
his hair before a family gathering

Matrimoney
Wedding gift

Manny
Live-in male babysitter

Weldding
Romantic event where two people pledge to be bonded for life

Manniversary
Annual celebration of gay marriages

Preteension
Vanity of the very young

Husbland
A dull married man

Prepaired
An arranged marriage

Minimom
The smallest degree of mothering permissible under law

Kinfants
Baby cousins

"You can get much farther with a kind word and a gun than you can with a kind word alone."

—Al Capone

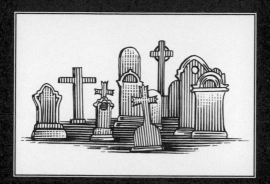

SCAMERAMEN
& CORONERSTONES
(CRIME & DEATH)

Deadication
In honor of someone who has passed on

Decomposse
Break up a large group of lawmen

Ghostel
Lodging for dead young people

Gulpability
Blame for swallowing evidence

Scameraman
One who takes pictures for blackmail

Mobligation
Debt owed to the Mafia

Pursecution
Accused of stealing a handbag

Discurnment
The ability to recognize one ash from another

Sharecopper
*A policeman whose salary is paid by
the people who have hired him*

Mobsession
Never missing an episode of "The Sopranos"

Carpus delicti
The "big one" that got away

Ghostage
A spirit held earthbound against its will

Insineration
A technique for destroying the evidence of a transgression

Coronerstone
Grave marker

Hemogoblin
A blood-sucking monster

Guillotwine
*The rope used by an executioner to lift a
blade into position for a beheading*

Mobservation
Gangland stakeout

Juxtaposse
In the Old West, a group of lawmen riding in close formation

Warrent
A legal document authorizing a search of a rabbit's home

Contrabrand
*Smuggled goods produced by a single
manufacturer and identified by name*

Maniacle
Handcuffs for the criminally insane

Orbituary
Notice of the death of a star

Honorabble
A mob worthy of respect

Massassination
St. Valentine's Day, Chicago, 1929

Cosa Noostra
A hanging rope used by the mob

MUSCELLANY
(MORE WORDS)

Canastrophe
A disastrous card game

Metrognome
A bus-riding, timekeeping dwarf

Thinterland
A remote fat farm

Castroturf
Cuban ground

Jubilante
A joyful poker stake

Astrollogy
A walk under the stars

Tumblesweed
A Scandinavian gymnast

Winterference
A snowstorm during a Thanksgiving Day parade

Dentonation
A common result of a punch thrown by boxer Mike Tyson

Psychick
Female fortune teller

Knightmare
Lancelot's bad dream

Shenanagan
A mischievous trick played on a grandmother

Nanagram
One billionth of a grandmother

Bookeeper
*One who keeps a record of the number of
negative responses during a baseball game*

Intheritance
Something passed on somewhere else

Covernant
*A formal agreement between bedmates
not to steal the blankets*

Prowpitious
A yacht favored to win a race by a nose

Petrolman
Gas station security guard

Inflatuation
An exuberant love of breaking wind

Hikerarchy
The order in which one climbs

Monolithe
A massive yet somehow graceful structure

Exodust
In ancient Egypt, an indication of departing Israelites

Pilgrimace
Life viewed as a painful journey

Muscellany
A variety of strong stuff

Chubcaps
Convex wheel covers

Mexiclan
A large Latino family

Matadoor
Entrance to a bull ring

Franchaise
A formal authorization to sell reclining chairs

Pectorial
Photo spread in a muscle magazine

Flossil
*A short length of petrified waxed thread
discovered beneath a bed*

Vehickle
An automobile driven by Lil Abner

Carate
Martial art for jewelers

Neanderthaw
The melting of an ancient ice man

Pillgrimage
A long drive to the pharmacy

Sparasol
Extra umbrella

Incalcuttable
*A city in eastern India with a population
too dense to be estimated*

Orbait
The path of a fishing worm around a pond

Bamboom
Explosion in a rattan furniture factory

Cabooze
The bar car

Thurdle
*The last of three barriers over which men
or horses must jump in a race*

Coinversation
Speaking to someone over a pay phone

Opiñata
Batting around an idea

Allbino
Inarguably pale

Caɛtush
Accidentally sitting on a succulent